T0129986

I don't give a f**k

Michael R Ransom

BALBOA.
PRESS
A DIVISION OF HAY HOUSE

Balboa Press books may be ordered through booksellers or by contacting:

Balboa Press
A Division of Hay House
1663 Liberty Drive
Bloomington, IN 47403
www.balboapress.com.au
1 (877) 407-4847

Because of the dynamic nature of the Internet, any web addresses or
links contained in this book may have changed since publication and
may no longer be valid. The views expressed in this work are solely those
of the author and do not necessarily reflect the views of the publisher,
and the publisher hereby disclaims any responsibility for them.

The author of this book does not dispense medical advice or prescribe the use
of any technique as a form of treatment for physical, emotional, or medical
problems without the advice of a physician, either directly or indirectly. The
intent of the author is only to offer information of a general nature to help
you in your quest for emotional and spiritual well-being. In the event you use
any of the information in this book for yourself, which is your constitutional
right, the author and the publisher assume no responsibility for your actions.

Any people depicted in stock imagery provided by Thinkstock are
models, and such images are being used for illustrative purposes only.
Certain stock imagery © Thinkstock.

Print information available on the last page.

ISBN: 978-1-5043-0454-2 (sc)
ISBN: 978-1-5043-0455-9 (e)

Balboa Press rev. date: 10/18/2016

Contents

Contents

Preface

This is my fifth book, my previous four books have all been to do with the automotive field, so a side step for me in terms of content, but If I were not to write this book, where else would you find the information I have spent a life time gathering. As I am a senior citizen meaning I have been around for a long time, meaning, long enough to see what is really going on and I feel the need to explain to people the truth about what is going on on planet earth The truth is out there, but most people have no clue where to look to find it. This book will tell you in plain English and I will not shy away from the truth, however unbelievable it may seem to some people.

Let us Talk About the Word Fuck

The word fuck is believed to have originated from the German word "flicken" meaning to strike and to better illustrate this I have included the following.

As a transitive verb, Bill fucked Elizabeth.

As an intransitive verb, Elizabeth fucks.

As an objective, Peter is doing all the fucking work.

As an adverb, Lynette talks too fucking much.

As an adverb enhancing an adjective, Anne is fucking beautiful.

As a noun, I don't give a fuck.

As part of a word, that's infuckingcredible.

Fraud, I was fucked over in that deal at the car yard.

Statement, I am really fucked now.

Difficulty, I don't understand this fucking question.

Inquiry, who the fuck was that.

Dissatisfaction, I don't like what the fuck is going on here

Trouble, I guess I am really fucked now

And finally to have sex, and we are not talking about making love, fucking someone is not the same, I think you know what I mean.

Now that we all agree what a fantastic descriptive word fuck is, we can turn our attention to the problem and how to solve it.

Chapter One

The Problem

Of course a large majority of the western world don't even realise there is a problem, they are too uneducated or too fucking stupid to have any clue what the fuck is happening around them, let alone realise any potential danger that is lurking around the corner.

The problem is so fucking obvious to me at least but I will spell it out, their is simply too many people on this planet, we only have 31% land mass with a percentage of that unsuitable for supporting life, due to deserts, flood plains, mountains etc, while the other 69% is covered in salt water. Check out the website "the world population" currently (late 2016) 7.4 billion. So what you say, well I have to admit maths was not my strongest subject at school but the days of one plus one equals two are long gone. Western families have typically 2 to 3 children, straight away we can see that the original number is compounding and say mom and dad have become grandparents, their children have had children, so in the space of a lifetime,

2 people have become a possible 14 and I am being conservative. How about all the third world countries, no fucking brains in most of those countries otherwise they would not be third world countries.

The continent of Africa is the source of most of the problem. Take Ethiopia for example, years ago the Brits were over on that part of the world and realised these poor unfortunate people were having an horrific problem with infant mortality. The thinking of the Ethiopians was to keep on having children because the more they had the greater chance that more would survive, making the family more prosperous. Being a first world country the Brits rushed in to help, great work chaps, pat the Brits on the back for helping their fellow man in need - wrong - introducing medical care programs and training people to better manage their own kind was very successful, in fact too successful, the mortality rate dropped dramatically, therefore the average family of approx 6 to 8 ballooned to 10 to 13 a new problem arose, how to feed all the extra mouths. Well, just clear more land and plant more crops, but then the monsoon rains come and because of the extra land clearing removing all the trees etc all the top soil and their crops are washed away - instant famine, so then the Brits have to spend a lot more money on food aid to help the starving nation, like a dog chasing its tail.

This is why I don't give to charities that specialise in helping these poor wretches, on the surface that might sound a little harsh, but if I give and all of my fellow countrymen also give, all we are doing is adding fuel to the fire, a few months of food aid will not dent my bank account, it will get the family in question over the winter and hopefully with a season will bring a good crop and all will be ok and in the mean time mum has pumped out yet another child so the poverty cycle continues. Of course the real problem was never the mortality rate, it was and still is, that all their spare time is spent fucking and typically (this is a world wide trend for black people) these people are not monogamous, they may be married but it I still quite acceptable to fuck around. I am sure white men would think this is a great idea and if you are smart make it work for you, but black men can't see past the end of their cocks and hence the problem.

Still on the subject of Ethiopia, I saw a documentary on TV how a few good hearted people from Tasmania in Australia had spent a year or two teaching the locals how to dig wells, I was amazed, these people have been living in the same land for a millennium and are not smart enough to figure out how to dig a fucking well. How the fuck they have survived this long is truly amazing, maybe a ready supply of fresh drinking water is a lower priority than a ready supply of pussy.

Why do you think AIDS has been so prolific in that continent? I was talking to a young Caucasian woman recently and the subject came up about black people and she admitted to being married to a black man. The conversation became interesting when she stated that she had done a lot of research in the area of why black people don't achieve and still live hand to mouth when white people have made fantastic advances in all things and it all boils down to the black people or the third world people are basically hunter gatherers and the white man is the warrior.

Even in a country like the USA which with a population approaching 330 million, with a black population 15% of that figure, see a similar trend with some black girls having a number of children, each with a different father and that has proven to be the single most common reason why black children living in the US today in a family without a male parent will commit crime and start the life cycle and as soon as they become old enough to go to an adult gaol will spend a large portion of their lives behind bars and did I mention 48% of people in gaol are black - what a fuckup. In hind site we are all smarter, but white America must surely regret bringing in all those slaves years ago and to think they had a 3 year war to decide what to do about them.

The solution is obvious, and I am not saying this is the only way to fix the problem, but the whole world must adopt a one-child policy. It has been quite successful in China with births down to just over a million a week, Thailand also has a similar plan in place and I commend them for showing the guts to do it. China really did not have a choice after that fucking idiot Mayo Zedong almost fucked the country by himself.

If we keep going the way we are, basic items like food and water will become scarcer, the amount of countries that live year to year on aid will increase to the point that mass starvation will be a regular occurrence.

Of course all the liberals are screaming that precious resources like corn for example is being converted into ethanol for use as fuel in motor vehicles. In the USA all gasoline products available from the gas station have a degree of ethanol in them, the farmers are happy to receive a stable income, yet the science says that the effort required to turn corn into ethanol is so great there is no net gain and the only reason that they use corn is because more corn is grown in the USA than anything else. Sugar cane is a much better choice and scientists now tell us that the greatest source of raw material for the manufacture of bio fuels is algae, who would have thought that the green slime that you see in ponds could be so useful. Another great idea in theory but in practice did not really pan out and once something like this is in place it is harder to repeal than it was to install in the first place.

In Japan it will not be a problem, there the population is falling, women have decided that they want change and are sick and tired of following in their mothers foot steps where they marry and start producing a family and spend the greater portion of their life looking after them. These women are embracing a career, and in doing so are marrying later in life or not marrying at all. More power to them I say and in fact one Japanese mathematician has calculated when the last person will die in that country.

Italy is also concerned about a reduced birth rate, smaller villages are becoming deserted as the younger people head for the big cities for work, and in some instances young couples are offered cash incentives to stay put.

In Europe, people from what were referred to as Eastern Block countries and Arabic countries, are flooding into the more affluent countries at an alarming rate, trying to avoid conflict or sick of their shitty peasant lifestyle, the internet has shown them what life can be like for them, putting pressure on many of these countries and their resources. Most of europe is now seeing the early results of this mass migration as everyone that ever thought that they wanted a better life has taken it upon themselves to make the move and the inevitable is happening with a sharp rise in crime and in particular crimes against women. A lot of these so called refugees or as I would call them opportunists are muslins who believe that women are second class citizens and have no respect or empathy for them, so the end result is women are being raped at an alarming rate. Back in their own shitty countries had they been caught they may have been executed, but in so called civilized countries where there is no sharia law or death penalty, their answer is to return these scumbags to the country that they came from.

Chapter Two

The Hidden Problem

It is obvious there was never going to be just one single problem that left us in the shit we are in, the hidden problem is all the small things that may go unnoticed but combine to create a major head fuck.

On the top of my hit list is religion, and this has been a problem for several thousand years with an upturn 2016 years ago, followed by a second wave 1476 years ago. Up until year zero, mad people believed in all sorts of shit, the sun, the moon and just about anything tangible, that people believed would give them some solace or hope or a cure for whatever ailed them. Some races even got carried away with their own beliefs, that they started killing animals to offer as a gift to their particular god, by chance, what they may have been praying for happened, it could have been something quite innocent but a link was formed between what the individual wanted so it was obvious to these people that the sacrifice worked. If the sacrifice did not work, maybe the gods were unhappy with this individual, maybe killing the goat was seen as too trivial, maybe 2 or 3 goats would be better, the individual did not want to appear to be ungrateful for all the help the gods had passed his way on previous occasions, then you look at the Aztec's, smart people that soon realised that goats were more valuable than some of the general population, so off with their heads instead.

2016 years ago Jesus was born in Bethlehem and spent most of his short life living in Nazareth and decided working as a carpenter was never going to make him rich and famous and whether he was smoking some good weed or whatever the case may be, got into his head that he should start his own religion, he ranted and raved trying to convince everyone that he was the son of god and therefore the king of the Jews until he picked up some followers and was all set to cash in when the local authorities were approached by the then leaders of the Jewish community complaining about this upstart making all sorts of claims. The local Roman governor at the time put the guy on trial, but because he had not broken any laws could not find him guilty, the Jewish leaders continued to complain so he was arrested again and this time found guilty and figuring he was a disruptive influence, so the local Roman governor decided to make an example of him by crucifying him. As luck would have it he did become dead famous, but sadly missed out on the riches.

The first hard copies of the guys demise were first written down 30 years after his death and you do not have to be a rocket scientist to realise that in the passing of time when the general population were illiterate the story was passed from person to person verbally with the odd omission or addition to make the story more colourful. As the story goes the body was dumped in a small cave with a large rock placed over the entrance to keep the rubber necks and grave robbers away and after three days the large rock had been moved and Jesus walks out. He then spends the next 40 days touring Israel talking up the benefits of believing in him and then in front of 11 of his disciples floats up into the air on his way to heaven, claiming "I'll be back" (to be with his heavenly father, god) if you believe that story you probably also believe in the tooth fairy. In this period it was common practice to store the bones of deceased family members in a stone crucible, which were then stored in underground caverns, and there were extensive caverns in the general Jerusalem area. Fast forward to the 1980's and the city limits of Jerusalem have expanded to the point where the caverns are being emptied of all these crucibles and relocated to the local university so the caverns can be filled in to make way for new housing. Years pass and eventually some guy gets the job of sorting out and cataloguing the hundreds of crucibles and one day he finds one with the dead famous guys name and his wife chiselled on the side of it. This is a significant find and after telling the various authorities of one of the greatest finds in modern times the church is informed with predictable alarm as they go into lock down to preserve cushy lifestyles with comments like "he is risen" meaning he went to heaven nearly 2000 years ago, how could these bones be his, yea right, more of that tooth fairy shit.

As I have said before people want something to believe in, people derive comfort from the belief that someone is looking out for them, their is this big book of instructions telling you everything you need to know to get by, how fucking lucky are we that a bunch of this guys friends sat down and spelled it out for us years later and of course if we have any problem with the interpretation or meaning of any part of the book their are people who's job it is to explain it to you, I know that must give a lot of people a warm and fuzzy feeling inside. The bible has been fucked with a lot in the early years with additions and subtractions over a long period and then of course it was originally written in Hebrew and with all translations words are changed or meanings altered just to add more confusion to a tall story.

Centuries ago most people were illiterate, people were fearful of the unknown so the smartest guy in the village became the local priest, think of the respect you could expect to receive if you could read and write and have the village in the palm of your hand because you were the one guy in the village who's job it was to interpret "the book", the power these people had in the community was amazing. Today there is over 100 different religions on this planet, back in the period we are discussing there were only a few and the one causing a lot of the problems which we are still dealing with today are those fucking

Catholics. The Spanish were quite prolific a few centuries ago touring the planet in their sailing ships conquering new lands offering these savages the opportunity to become catholic or die. As the numbers of Catholics around the planet started to grow so did the wealth of the church. And when the priest died his family expected to and did inherit some of the property and artefacts etc that the priest had acquired, but after awhile the church could see they were losing ground, literally, so a decision was made in the 11th century with the outcome being that priests were not allowed to marry their fore could not take a wife, could not have children and the church's real estate and artefacts were safe again.

In the 16th and 17th century a major problem descended on Europe, the black plague, a disease carried by rats infecting humans at an alarming rate because the population were ignorant at the time of basic hygiene. For whatever reason more men died than women leaving a lot of women on their own, and what do women like to do when they have some spare time, get together and talk, nothing has changed and it is in their DNA and at the end of the day who gives a fuck, the Catholic church certainly did. And that was the start of the period known as the inquisition. The pope, who had told the priests no more fucking around decided there was something going on here that they should know about, so he told "gods travelling salesmen" to find out what subversive activities these women were really up to. So they decide to interview a few of these women to find out what is really going on.

Well nothing was going on - wrong answer - after a little torture some of the women confessed, some refused so a second interview was conducted most at this point did confess and the stubborn ones who still refused to confess to doing nothing wrong were interviewed a third time which killed them and this is where the modern term comes from of the first, second and third degree, people do not like to be tortured so it was not surprising that people would dob in a neighbour, friend or even a family member to ease their pain. In one instance in England a whole village was euthanized as one dobbed on some one who dobbed on some else. It was quite obvious to the priests that witchcraft was behind all this subversive activity so burning these poor women at the stake was a great way of getting rid of the evidence while cleansing their souls with fire at the same time and in England it was estimated that more than 2000 women were killed this way.

Hopefully all this nasty shit has been forgotten about and the catholic church can go about gods work (not sure exactly what that is) with their heads held high - wrong - in these modern times communication has been a major growth area so we do not need to be told by another person what is going on in the world, we have telephones, TV, computer etc, so any little secret you are hiding has the potential to be public knowledge. The problem is paedophilia, and this is not isolated to an area or even a country, this is a problem world wide and of course the priests realised what an abundant resource of arse was available free for the taking, it has gotten so bad that a significant percentage of men joining the priesthood were in fact paedophiles and to go through all the religious mumbo jumbo to get all that free arse was well worth it.

Another weird thing that only Catholics believe in is saints, to think for a moment that praying is anything but a total waste of time and to think that if you have an ailment and you pray to a dead person and you get better, the dead person you prayed to should be bestowed the title of saint, so everyone else can pray to them as well and get better, I personally put more trust in our medical system.

Infact I recently spoke to a guy who I have had the odd business dealing with over the years, nice enough guy, but a Christian fundamentalist so approach with caution, anyway we can have fun debating his fucked up way of thinking and he tells me his older brother is dying of prostate cancer, and then he tells me that his brother has prayed and prayed, infact the whole family has prayed for god to spare him. God was on vacation at the time so his brother is fucked, you would think that in these modern times that he would have wanted medical intervention, but not so, they prayed even harder and I suppose when he does die, the family will think that god had a special plan for him and needed him upstairs asap. The guy is 65 years old, but in these modern times with quality medical care we are living longer and he probably missed out on 15 years of life and all the benefits that go along with that.

The other religion on my hit list are the Muslims, Muhammad was born in Mecca in 570 ad and at age 40 decides he needs to be the centre of attention by telling anyone who will listen that he is a prophet and that the angel Gabriel visited him in a dream which continued for 23 years until his death and is talking to him and only he can hear him. Armed with all of the knowledge to form his own religion he has written it down for everyone to read and it's called the Quran. This guy is trying to muscle in on the local religions at the time but in 622 ad he is forced to flee to Medina having pissed off the local authorities to the point that they want him dead, and having only moderate success anyway in Mecca with approx 100 followers. During the next ten years he steps up his efforts to gain religious control, infidels were either evicted or enslaved, converted upon point of death or slaughtered all in the name of Allah, and to fund his religion he would have his followers raid Meccano caravans having provided them with convenient revelations "from Allah" which allowed them to murder innocent drivers and steal their property, including wives and children.

At this time until his death in 632ad he continues to raise his profile by ordering assassinations on people he felt were in his way and doing battle with tribes, offering them the option of becoming Muslim or dying and is certainly no stranger to getting blood on his hands, and is remembered for being a murderer, rapist & a paedophile. I thought the Catholics were bad but the Muslims take it to a whole new level, believing the ravings of a madman that lived nearly 1500 years ago, and for some unexplained reason a small percentage of fundamentalists have taken it upon themselves to create havoc for the rest of the people sharing this planet. Now after a couple of wars in the middle east there is a new country started by these halfwits called ISIS where the people in charge want to run their empire the way it would have been run 1500 years ago, apart from the obvious problem that you cannot turn back time or the populations mindset, the only way they can control the population is through fear and oppression. In other words they have created a Muslim dictatorship, this is not a religion. To think that by killing a non Muslim or infidels as we are referred to as gets them extra points in heaven and a bunch of virgins thrown in as a bonus shows the mentality of these people. If it was not for crude oil under a significant portion of the middle east all the shit that we are dealing with for the last twenty + years would not have happened and when it eventually runs out they can go back to fucking camels and leave the rest of the world to sort out its own problems.

In my opinion Muhammad was just another attention seeking individual who was more than happy to get blood on his hands to get people to take him seriously, who lived in a period in history where his fellow man was basically illiterate who came up with a great idea to make him rich and famous (sound familiar) and ran with it. Being a super salesman certainly helped and who would have thought that today this idiot's legacy would be so prolific.

Recently I saw a documentary (made in France) about young Muslims, basically a French journalist (Arab) went undercover for 6 months to see what was really going on and report on his findings. This journalist mixed with these losers enough to gain their trust and at the end informed the authorities before they had a chance to create any more havoc than France has recently experienced. While planning their attack on the innocent French people, this arsehole was explaining to the journalist (via a hidden camera) how the palace in paradise was so large that if you stood in front of it you could not see from one side to the other and you could not count the number of virgins waiting around to offer themselves to these losers. Then this arsehole makes a statement that "I am not making this shit up" had me rolling around on the floor laughing, what a fucked up mind set these people have, can't wait to blow themselves up for a fucked up cause and no appreciation of life and the rights of other people living on this planet. And what about the innocent Muslims that get killed when the target is really infidels, they get a quick one way trip to paradise which we all now know has a huge mansion and lots of virgins to fuck, so they have done the individual a favour by killing him, these people are fucked in the head.

Scientology certainly has certainly put a different spin on religion, founded in 1954 by Ron Hubbard who was visited by an alien one day, and in conversation imparted all this information, which would be very handy if you wanted to start your own religion. Ron not wanting to look a gift horse in the mouth did just that and for a fee (after joining the sect of course) you will go through a intensive course to rid any issues you may have to cleanse your mind of everything (that is worrying you) so you can be re programmed to be a model scientologist and I should mention that in the USA they have tax free status, so the old statement of a sucker born every minute has made the church of scientology very wealthy.

Once of the last guy to try and claim prophet status last century was Vernon Howell, a dyslexic son born to a 14 year old girl in 1959 who was raised by his grandparents and was going no where fast until he joined the Branch Davidians. Wrestling control in 1988 after a gun fight with the current leader and later changing his name to David Koresh (Persian for Cyrus the Great) wows his disciples with guitar in hand and of course being the divine one allowed him to have sex with all females in the sect and it all comes to a head in 1993 in a predictable shit fight with the authorities where they all commit suicide and burn down their compound with their bodies still inside leaving little evidence of another failed attempt by an individual to change the world.

Through history their has been many people who have claimed to have either super natural powers or who ever or what ever they claim to be is pure bullshit. In western society they nearly always claim to be a re-incarnated Jesus and I think from memory last century there were several at the same time. The problem exists because a small percentage of the population are either born with or develop a mental condition and throw in a little religion and bingo another saviour is created, this people start ranting and raving and before long a bunch of gullible individuals have joined their cause believing that if they stick with this individual they will be saved.

Chapter Three

God What God

Most people if asked and answer honestly do believe in a god, depending on your brand of religion your god may look different to the next guys god, they all do the same thing and centuries after mankind started to roam this planet they still derive comfort in the knowledge that someone is looking out for them. Well I might as well tell you now rather than later that god is a man made phenomenon, he is (generally referred to as masculine) a figment of someone's imagination a long time ago, and like a lot of things that we grow up with, you tend to believe it when everyone around you, your parents, grandparents teachers etc all believe it then it must be true - wrong - then our whole fabric of society must be based on lies, yes, but why, "control" of course the priest has control of his flock as gods representative here on planet earth, you need guidance or questions about most things the priest has the answer, he is an educated guy remember.

Our universe is believed to be 13.7 billion years old and this planet was like most other planets a lump of hot rock floating around in space, nothing to see here, eventually it cools down and due to the fact of the proximity of the planet within our solar system mainly the distance from the sun and that we have a moon an atmosphere is created, this does not go unnoticed by the guys who really look after this planet, you would refer to them as aliens (a person born of another race or of another world) having planet earth finally come of age meant they could visit on a regular basis and try out some ideas. Most of the living things on this planet were brought here in some form or another, back up for a moment to explain how this works which is not that much different that how things work on this planet. In a civilised western country you have a government and because the country has numerous states you have state governments as well, look at this in a larger format, you have a planet inhabited by aliens who controls several smaller planets obviously run by aliens just like here except because they so much smarter than us and look funny compared to what we are used to seeing, and we would be intimidated by them. Anyway the teacher asks his students one day as a project to design a life form that must be self sustaining and be able to survive in a given environment, the students diligently work away at this task until they are ready for field trials and you guessed it planet earth. Some work better than others some of them might need a tune up to get the design right and some don't do too much at all and become extinct.

The next year another class of students get the opportunity to do the same thing and eventually planet earth is looking green and life forms are doing well, well most of them, some of the larger clumsy looking creatures with relatively small brains for the size of their body were eliminated as they were not intelligent enough to adapt, don't forget earth time and alien time are not the same and the same format is trialled over millions of earth years with mankind just another experiment. Thousands of years ago man was not so aggressive towards the visitors from space with the continent South America covered in rock art etc depicting what they saw.

Fast forward to the middle of last century, people start seeing things in the sky, what the fuck is this shit they say, are we under attack, what a fucking joke. As man has finally become sophisticated enough (not smart enough) to blow up the planet killing all who live on it the aliens become concerned that all the work they did creating life on this planet we are going to turn it into a radio active wasteland. Hollywood catches onto the idea and before you know it movies are playing in the cinema's showing aliens attacking us and I have seen TV shows in 2015 which for the correct terminology escapes me I will call them bullshit documentaries still on about these aliens attacking us. I thought airtime was expensive and to be served up this shit on the TV is beyond belief, but I guess I had the option to change channels. Maybe I should explain that the more sophisticated a society becomes acts of aggression, violence etc diminish. This type of behaviour is not what drives these aliens, we have nothing to fear and I for one would embrace the opportunity to mingle with them, think for a moment what they could teach us if we lower our weapons long enough to listen to what they had to say.

That is why they visit in the dark of night, no one wants to become a target and even though their spacecraft is more sophisticated than we could possible understand a lucky shot could reach its target. I am sure there are people who work for government agencies around the planet, who deliberately withhold information to the general public to ensure that the status quo remains intact. Remember how we all think their is a god and that aliens are bullshit, what is going to happen if the truth ever gets out, will our society survive from the centuries of bullshit fed to us by the church and politicians, all for our own good of course.

Every time there is a major problem on this planet the sightings increase as the aliens come for a closer look to see what these fuckwits on planet earth are up to this time. During the second world war allied pilots reported balls of light near the ends of the wings of their planes followings the planes from England to Europe on bombing raids, not all the time but it did become a common occurrence (infect they were alien drones, and the allies originally thought they were a new type of German weapon, and it was later revealed that German pilots saw them too) sometimes the pilot would flip his wings to push the ball away, but each time they would move out of the way so a collision would not occur and then settle down in their usual place just above the end of the wing and these balls of light became known as Foo Fighters, and you thought that was an original name for a rock band.

Scientists in a vague attempt to explain this phenomenon have labelled such things as ball lightning, something that has been observed on a rare occasion when the atmosphere has to be just right and in an attempt to put a label on it I am sure such things do actually exist, but what was described by airmen during the second world war is not what scientist claim is ball lightning.

I personally know a guy of a similar age to myself that was with a bunch of friends working on a friends race car one night when nature called and while a distance from the workshop saw an alien drone a short distance away, he yelled out to his friends in the workshop to come quickly to see what was happening, twelve people stood in awe as this drone which essentially was a ball approx 3 ft in diameter rapidly change colour turning on its own axis clockwise and counter clockwise backwards and forwards essentually showing off to these guys and then in an instant it was gone. Upon reflection everyone agreed that they all saw the same thing all though most had no clue what it was and in subsiquent days some of the guys would not discuss the matter and some even doubted that they saw anything.

In 1969 when man finally broke free of earth's gravity and headed towards the moon the rocket was followed by an alien craft, when they finally landed on the moon the aliens also landed a half mile away to keep an eye on what we were doing and I would like to think they had a smile on their faces when they watched the astronauts try to move around in zero gravity. NASA was informed of their presence and were told to ignore them, probably the best opportunity we as a planet have been offered to make contact considering it was all being filmed and we blew it, how fucking typical is that.

Chapter Four

Am I Dead

Generally people are shit scared of dying, basically a fear of the unknown, easy to understand, recently someone was going through the archives of an old catholic church in England and found what appeared to be common practise centuries ago when the general population was illiterate and ignorant (more than today that is) and a certain person who was not a young man and no one lived to be a ripe old age then anyway, had paid the local priest a reasonable sum of money to ensure he would end up in heaven because the alternative was so shocking and no one wanted that, so a messenger had been sent to Rome to get the popes assurance that he would enter the kingdom of heaven when he died, as you could imagine travel back then was a slow and tedious exercise and when the messenger finally returned with the papers signed the man in question had already died, you can image the terror this guy was haunted with during his last days alive. Years ago the best way to keep you flock in toe was to have them fear all sorts of things hell was the big Cohuna of them all, was hell, and of course no one travelled so no one really new that all this stuff being spread by the church was bullshit. The word hell referred to a valley outside of Jerusalem called Hellum, a middle ages version of Soweto I expect and with a bit of bullshit thrown in and the old saying of don't let the truth get in the way of a good story and the churches coffers were always being topped up.

I find it hard to believe that almost everyone I speak to about death is quite categorical about what happens when you die, nothing is almost the universal reply, when I attempt to explain what is really going on their eyes glaze over or their ears fail to hear, I will admit my target audience are non religious people. Let me explain, as we are the highest on the food chain on planet earth we get the privilege of reincarnation, we live in a three dimensional world we have length, width and depth, before you were born you were selected for the couple that were to become your parents, why, to be brought up in a family that would give you the opportunities and skills to achieve whatever was predetermined for you to do, to make your life more fulfilling and to reach your goals. When your body is worn out and you die, your inner self or soul or whatever you want to call it continues on for another round. It is just like going to school you have passed grade one and come back to go through grade two and so on until you have finished school and then pass into the next dimension and the process starts all over again, and in a fourth dimension you wanted to go to another city or country, no more air travel just think it and you are there, and their are more dimensions after that.

So living in a third dimension we are just starting out with a lot to learn, so after dying and in a holding pattern until being reborn again will have a critical look back over the life you have just lived to see what a great job or how badly you fucked up. Like I said before, space time is different to planet earth time so you can relax and come to grips with your new surroundings, perhaps you were an axe murderer, we all go to the same place but next time you are reborn you may be the nicest person, very compassionate and in some way trying to make up for transgressions of a previous life. You may have decided that your life is not a happy one, perhaps you suffered from depression and decided it was all too hard and decided to commit suicide, definitely a mistake so instead of years of R&R straight back to school for you and because you did not complete the previous life and must make up for your past indiscretions meaning your next life could cut short maybe for no obvious reason to get back on track. Perhaps you made a few enemies in that past life, no you don't have to spend your R&R with eyes in the back of your head, if you don't want to meet with someone it will not happen.

I think it is a real shame that the general population does not have a better understanding about what they are doing here, if their is really such a thing as the meaning of life, I would suggest it is to be enthusiastic with whatever you are into, give it your best shot, work hard and respect you fellow man and I am sure if we all did this we would all get along better maybe a few less wars and less crime and speaking of crime because most western countries are smart and have access to technology I think as soon as someone is born they should be DNA tested and the records stored for at least their life time. I can already hear all the civil libertarians booing and hissing, but think about it for a moment, crime would be slashed as it is almost impossible to hide DNA at a crime scene and with everyone's DNA recorded bingo. The reason it is currently impossible to solve lots of crime because the DNA bank is almost empty, think about it people.

Another important benefit to DNA testing is medical profiling. Medicine has come along way in the last century but sadly its progress is being inhibited by people's appetite for reproduction over good sense. If a person is born with or a carrier of a problem disease it can be eliminated, prevention is always going to be better than the cure. As an example I saw a documentary on TV about an Australian family that had originally arrived in that country with the first fleet in 1788 and over a period of approx 220 years had the odd uncle or aunt that was a bit "funny" and died earlier than what the norm was at the time and the middle aged woman who was the subject of the story had gone to the doctor with a complaint and the doctor had referred her onto an expert and was subsequently DNA profiled to discover she was the carrier of a rare disease and having had the family tree in hand could spot all the previous family members that had also suffered from this disease. Obviously the whole family should be DNA tested and the ones carrying the markers sterilised to stop the disease in its tracks. Seem simple to me but the need to breed or a good fuck is all consuming and the old saying that a stiff dick has no conscience is also true. I can tell you from personal experience that not having children is not the end of the world, what it does do is allow the individual to expand his or her interests and explore more opportunities. Now that I am older, I am also suffering from a rare untreatable disease and while no other members of my family past of present appear to be affected, I can in hind site be thankful that I never had children thus eliminating the possibility of me passing on the disease to my children.

In some instances doctors can keep a patient alive for weeks, months and even years whether they want to or not, although in some instances I wonder if the doctor's bank account is more important than the patient's right to die.

Doctors are now saying they expect to be able to keep people alive until they are 150 years old, back to what I said previously about putting off death because you are scared of dying. With better medical care and diet people are certainly living a lot longer, but the problem remains that when you become old and all your friends and family die and you can't get around like you used to, so what is the up side of living to you are 150.

Here is a topic that seems to create havoc depending on your religious stand point, abortion, this would not be an issue if anyone had a fucking clue what goes on. Firstly just prior to when a child is born the soul of the child is installed in the child and when born the child then has the characteristics we all know and understand. Had the child been aborted at an earlier time this does not happen, when the child is born and it is outside the mothers womb it is of course a living being, abortions are carried out quite early in the pregnancy and are not capable of living /breathing on their own, they are a foetus not a child and by aborting one for whatever reason is not murder. Only a couple of decades ago in Russia which was and still is to some degree a backward country with limited birth control measures in place offered women abortions for unwanted pregnancies some women had up to ten of them without any ill effect. So my message to the right to life movement is "fuck off".

I will make a brief comment on Darwin's theory of evolution, and he would be right in some small part in that a creature leaving in a given environment will over time adapt to that environment, but overall looking at the big picture I cannot agree with his theory and if you think for a second that man evolved from an ape you are fucking crazy, sure our DNA sequence is very similar but to think we "evolved" from one to the other is madness, we were designed to be what we are, sure we are not the perfect model, maybe there are other races on other planets which were created after us that have better design features so they do not get sick, purely speculation on my part.

One of the most stupid ideas to come out of the later part of the 20th century must surely be cryogenics, when you die your whole body is snap frozen in liquid nitrogen, but that's expensive shit, so it was suggested that only the brain be frozen to save space and because the brain is delicate they decided to remove and freeze the whole head while waiting for a cure. What a fucking joke, anyone who put up money for this was seriously fucked over.

Chapter five

Cosmology Fact or Fiction

Cosmology/astronomy, in this day and age we are fed a continual stream of information regarding the latest theories on black holes, parallel universe's, big bang etc. In reality all this stuff is just theory and I am constantly amazed by all this stuff we are fed. I was blown away when a guy received the noble peace prize for showing on paper that the universe is expanding, I could have told him that but I would be unable to show how to calculated it and at the end of the day, so what! How does that help the plight of our fellow man? Another scientist took it upon himself to show what happened before the big bang, who gives a fuck what happened here more than 13.7 billion years ago, our planet is suffering real problems now and some scientist on a big salary is wasting resources on shit like this.

Here is another topic that pisses me off "Mars" the next planet in our solar system going away from the sun; the amount of hoopla about this piece of rock is really amazing. I constantly hear reference to this piece of rock on the TV every week, some one finds a small rock on the ground and obviously it has come from space, earth receives a continual shower of debris from space, so does almost every other planet, most of it burns up when it hits our atmosphere, we call the bigger ones shooting stars, but for some reason people think this is from Mars. Then the theory that life started on Mars and then transferred to earth, now scientists say there is water under Mars north pole, so what it is frozen, and now they have turned their attention to looking for any microscopic bacteria, then their is a group that want to travel to Mars on a one way trip to start colonization of this planet, enough of all this shit! Mars is a rock, like most of the other planets out there, the mineral content may differ slightly, but essentially it is still a rock, which being so far from the sun, temperatures can drop to around 90 degrees celcius below zero has strong winds and no atmosphere which means all the harmful rays the sun emits which we are shielded from on planet earth because we have an atmosphere does not exist on Mars, so you will not be able to go outside for more than two hours a day and because we are running out of room on earth is no reason to contemplate colonizing another planet. With our current crude technology it would take approx 6 months to get there and humans don't do too well just travelling in space for long periods of time, maybe we should look after this planet a lot better and the need to move can be avoided.

How about that always-smiling Brit scientist, Brian Cox, obviously an intelligent guy, but has trouble seeing the wood for the trees. I saw him being interviewed live on TV and a member of the audience mentioned that he had seen a UFO and observed its movements for approx 5 minutes, Brian said, no you did not and without breaking his sentence continued about something else. I find it amazing that so called intelligent well educated people like this guy and their are a lot of them out there refuse to believe that their are other people living their lives in a similar way we do on other planets, scientists tell us their are more planets out in space than their are grains of sand on all the beaches on planet earth and yet we are the only planet inhabited is a fucking joke. In the USA the SETI institute sends out signals via radio waves into outer space trying to make contact with other life forms, yet the USA government hides the fact that they have already made contact years ago.

The Hubble telescope has shown mankind that their is so much more out there than we ever thought possible and what we are now seeing is only the tip of the iceberg, so expand your thoughts people to the possibilities of all sorts of things that are going on that we are not aware of.

The old saying that "if you can't root, shoot or electrocute" something it does not exist is bullshit.

If we go back 120 years it was thought that man could not survive driving a motor car faster than 30 mph and yet nearly 20 years ago a car was driven at 763 mph (speed of sound) and a couple of teams are racing to build a car to reach 1000 mph.

So to conclude, all I can hope for is that you have learned something and enjoyed reading this as much as I did writing it and open your mind to possibilities that until now you may not have realised existed. For the sceptics, I cannot physically prove what I claim is fact, but when you die all will be revealed.

About the Author

This is my fifth book, the previous four have been about my involvement in the automotive field, so a side step for me in terms of content, but if I were not to write this book where else would you find the information I have spent a life time gathering.

Printed in the United States
By Bookmasters